KT-467-497

Slow Cooker

Everyday recipes to enjoy

GALWAY COUNTY LIBRARIES

Bath • New York • Singapore • Hong Kong • Cologne • Delhi
Melbourne • Amsterdam • Johannesburg • Shenzhen

tomato & lentil soup

ingredients

SERVES 4

2 tbsp sunflower oil

1 onion, chopped

1 garlic clove, finely chopped

2 celery sticks, chopped

2 carrots, chopped

1 tsp ground cumin

1 tsp ground coriander

175 g/6 oz red or yellow lentils

1 tbsp tomato purée

1.2 litres/2 pints vegetable
    stock

400 g/14 oz canned
    chopped tomatoes

1 bay leaf

salt and pepper

crème fraîche and toasted
    crusty bread, to serve

method

1 Preheat the slow cooker, if necessary, or according to the manufacturer's instructions.

2 Heat the oil in a saucepan. Add the onion and garlic and cook over a low heat, stirring occasionally, for 5 minutes, or until softened. Stir in the celery and carrots and cook, stirring occasionally, for a further 4 minutes. Stir in the ground cumin and coriander and cook, stirring, for 1 minute, then add the lentils.

3 Mix the tomato purée with a little of the stock in a small bowl and add to the pan with the remaining stock, the tomatoes and bay leaf. Bring to the boil, then transfer to the slow cooker. Stir well, cover and cook on low for 3½–4 hours.

4 Remove and discard the bay leaf. Transfer the soup to a food processor or blender and process until smooth. Season to taste with salt and pepper. Ladle into warmed soup bowls, top each with a swirl of crème fraîche and serve immediately with toasted crusty bread.

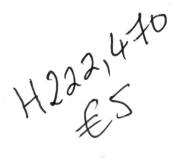

chicken & dumplings

ingredients

SERVES 4

2 tbsp olive oil

1 large onion, thinly sliced

2 carrots, cut into 2-cm/
   $^3/_4$ -inch chunks

225 g/8 oz French beans,
   cut into 2.5-cm/1-inch
   lengths

4 skinless, boneless chicken
   breasts

300 ml/10 fl oz hot chicken
   stock

salt and pepper

dumplings

200 g/7 oz self-raising flour

100 g/$3^1/_2$ oz shredded suet

4 tbsp chopped fresh parsley

method

1 Preheat the slow cooker, if necessary, or according to the manufacturer's instructions.

2 Heat 1 tablespoon of oil in a frying pan, add the onion and fry over a high heat for 3–4 minutes, or until golden. Place in the slow cooker with the carrots and beans.

3 Add the remaining oil to the pan, then add the chicken breasts and fry until golden, turning once. Arrange on top of the vegetables in a single layer, season well with salt and pepper and pour over the stock. Cover and cook on low for 4 hours.

4 Turn the slow cooker up to high while making the dumplings. Sift the flour into a bowl and stir in the suet and parsley. Season to taste with salt and pepper. Stir in just enough cold water to make a fairly firm dough, mixing lightly. Divide into 12 and shape into small balls.

5 Arrange the dumplings on top of the chicken, cover and cook for 30 minutes on high. Serve immediately.

GALWAY COUNTY

GALWAY COUNTY LIBRARIES

pot roast with beer

ingredients

SERVES 4-6

2 small onions, each cut
    into 8 wedges

8 small carrots, halved
    lengthways

1 fennel bulb, cut into 8
    wedges

2.25 kg/5 lb rolled chuck steak

2 tbsp Dijon mustard

1 tbsp plain flour

100 ml/3$\frac{1}{2}$ fl oz beer

salt and pepper

method

1 Preheat the slow cooker, if necessary, or according to the manufacturer's instructions.

2 Place the onions, carrots and fennel in the slow cooker and season to taste with salt and pepper. Place the beef on top.

3 Mix the mustard and flour together to form a paste and spread over the beef. Season well and pour over the beer. Cover and cook on low for 8 hours.

4 Carefully remove the beef and vegetables and place on a warmed platter. Skim the excess fat from the juices and pour into a jug to serve with the beef.

GALWAY COUNTY LIBRARIES

This edition published by Parragon Books Ltd in 2013

Parragon Books Ltd
Chartist House
15–17 Trim Street
Bath BA1 1HA, UK
www.parragon.com

Copyright © Parragon Books Ltd 2010–2013

All rights reserved. No part of this publication may be reproduced, stored in a retrieval system or transmitted, in any form or by any means, electronic, mechanical, photocopying, recording or otherwise, without the prior permission of the copyright holder.

ISBN: 978-1-4723-2694-2

Printed in China

Notes for the Reader

This book uses both metric and imperial measurements. Follow the same units of measurement throughout; do not mix metric and imperial. All spoon measurements are level: teaspoons are assumed to be 5 ml, and tablespoons are assumed to be 15 ml. Unless otherwise stated, milk is assumed to be full fat, eggs and individual vegetables are medium, and pepper is freshly ground black pepper. Unless otherwise stated, all root vegetables should be washed in plain water and peeled prior to using.

Garnishes, decorations and serving suggestions are all optional and not necessarily included in the recipe ingredients or method.

The times given are an approximate guide only. Preparation times differ according to the techniques used by different people and the cooking times may also vary from those given. Optional ingredients, variations or serving suggestions have not been included in the time calculations.

Recipes using raw or very lightly cooked eggs should be avoided by infants, the elderly, pregnant women, convalescents and anyone suffering from an illness. Pregnant and breastfeeding women are advised to avoid eating peanuts and peanut products. Sufferers from nut allergies should be aware that some of the ready-made ingredients used in the recipes in this book may contain nuts. Always check the packaging before use.